Railways in Profile Se

BRITISH RAILWAY
PRIVATE OWNER WAGONS
OPENS and HOPPERS

Compiled by G.Gamble

CHEONA PUBLICATIONS

© 1999 Cheona Publications

ISBN 1900298 11 2

Production, design and setting by:
Print Rite, The Willows, School Lane,
Stadhampton, Oxford OX44 7TR

Printed by Alpha Print, Crawley, Oxon.

Published by:
Cheona Publications
39 The Avenue, Chinnor,
Oxfordshire 0X9 4PD

The Railways In Profile Series.
> No 1 British Railway Wagons. Opens and Hoppers.
> No.2 Great Western Stations.
> No.3 British Railway Vans.
> No.4 British Railway Wagons. Railtanks.
> No.5 British Railway Brake Vans and Cattle Wagons.
> No.6 British Railway Non-Passenger Rolling Stock.
> No.7 British Railway Wagons. Engineer's Stock - *Volume One*
> No.8 British Railway Engineer's Stock - *Volume Two*
> No.9 British Railway Private Owner Wagons -Opens and Hoppers.

Acknowledgements

Such a work as this relies heavily on the availability of photographs and grateful thanks are extended to all who have helped in this matter. They have been indicated by initials to each plate and are:-
R.B. - R. Blencowe, E.B. - Eric Bruton, R.C. - Roger Carpenter, P.C. - Phil Coutanche, B.D. - Brian Daniels, G.W.S./ N.B. - Great Western Society -Nick Baxter, B.H. - Bernard Holland, P.J. - Peter Jary, S.J. - Steve Jordan, D.L. - David Larkin, L. - Lens of Sutton, T.R. - Tim Rogers, J.S.M. - John Scott Morgan, R.S. - Roger Speller, A.T. - Alan Turner and H.F.W./R.C. - the late Hubert Wheeler (courtesy of Roger Carpenter).
Many of the above and other friends have assisted by answering questions and supplying further information for which I am most grateful. Bernard Holland, Alan Turner and Peter Merry deserve special thanks in this connection.

Preface

Like the earlier books in this series, this one looks at another aspect of post -1948 rolling stock history in the form of the private owner wagon, which has seen fluctuating fortunes on our railways. It was virtually banished after Nationalisation except for the non-pool wagons but after a revival which started in the 1970's , privatisation has seen a veritable plethora of new types.
I hope that the subjects chosen will appeal to modellers, wagon enthusiasts and historians alike. Some colour has been included in this volume but despite many enquiries and much searching it has not proved possible to find suitable colour photographs of early wagons especially the 'P' registered stock. Doubtless when this book is read someone out there will produce a box full!!

Useful references include :- 'Private Owner Wagons - *Volume 1*' by Andrew Marshall published by *Metro Enterprises* in 1992, ISBN 0 947773 22 3, 'Modern Private Owner Wagons on British Rail' by David Ratcliffe published by *PSL* in 1989, *(and currently out of print),* ISBN 1 85260 062 4, Leicester Railway Wagon Society's bi-monthly magazine - 'National Freight Scene' and from the same source 'Private Owner Wagons 1995' by Carl Cox.

Introduction

Privately owned wagons gave the railways a great variety of colour which lasted until the period of World War II. The majority of these wagons were coal carriers owned principally by collieries but these and many other private owner wagons were pooled by the Ministry of War Transport from 1939 and many were damaged beyond repair in the hostilities between 1939 and 1945. Despite the original intention, the survivors were never returned to their owners because the railways of Britain were Nationalised in 1948. British Railways instituted its own design and build programme and by 1958 most of the private owner wagons had been eliminated from the system apart from those specialised non-pool types like tank wagons, some of which were dealt with in *volume 4* in this series. The BR attitude mellowed however and by the early 1970's customers moving large quantities of material on a regular basis were encouraged to provide their own approved rolling stock and so private owner wagons began to appear again either company owned or hired or leased from the major hire companies which developed. Other factors encouraged private customers to use rail transport such as Government grants to cover 60% of the cost of new rolling stock and rail - accessed loading and unloading facilities, the development of Speedlink services and the TOPS coding and control of wagon distribution. Such has been the development of new private owner rolling stock since the early 1980's that only open and hopper wagons can be covered in this volume and even then some types such as bogie hoppers will need further consideration at a later date. Variations in the huge fleets of Foster Yeoman and Amey Roadstone have been given some degree of representative coverage but a complete volume could probably have been given over to these! Lengths of wagons quoted are given 'over buffers' unless stated otherwise.

The 1923 Railway Clearing House specification

The 'standard type' of private owner 12 ton open mineral wagon had various components such as buffers and brakegear which were interchangeable if repairs were necessary. It was built to standard dimensions being 6ft wide over headstocks with a 16ft 6ins long body. Three varieties were common:-

8 plank	8ft 9$\frac{1}{2}$ins tall above rail height	All 8 planks were 6$\frac{7}{8}$ins wide
7 plank	8ft 6$\frac{1}{4}$ins " "	5 planks 6$\frac{7}{8}$ins wide 2 *(top)* 8$\frac{7}{8}$ins wide
5 plank	7ft 3$\frac{1}{4}$ins " "	5 planks 7$\frac{3}{8}$ins wide.

When a steel underframe was used the sides fitted outside the floor and the overall height was 2$\frac{1}{2}$ins less. 7 and 8 plank wagons had side and end doors, (sometimes two end doors), 5 plank wagons had side doors only. 7 and 8 plank wagons could have bottom discharge doors which were indicated on post-1948 stock by a white 'V' on the centre of the side. All three types could have:-

1. Independent or Morton brakegear.   2. 'T' iron or wooden end stanchions.
3. Any of three types of axlebox :- 'Gloucester', (used by GW, SR and many private owners), LNER or LMS styles.
4. Plain, ribbed or self-contained buffers.   5. Steel or wooden underframes.

However, variations did occur in overall height, plank width and the positioning of the solebar fittings.

Abbreviations

AFI	Accelerator Freight Inshot		ICIM	Imperial Chemical Ind. Mond Division
APCM	Associated Portland Cement Manufacturers		OK	Orenstein & Koppel
ARC	Amey Roadstone		PR	Procor Ltd
BBC	Boothferry Borough Council		REDA	Redland Aggregates
BIS	British Industrial Sand		RLS	Railease
BREL	British Rail Engineering Ltd.		SRW	Standard Railway Wagon
BRT	British Railway Traffic & Electric Co.		STET	Steetley Refractories Ltd.
BSC	British Steel Corporation		TAMC	Tarmac Roadstone
BSSC	British Steel Corporation Scunthorpe		TCS	Tilling Construction
BSCO	British Steel Corporation Corby		THOM	Thompson Quarries Ltd.
BSGL	British Steel Corporation Glasgow		TOPS	Total Operations Processing System
BSSH	British Steel Corporation Shotton		TRL	Tiger Rail Ltd.
BSSW	British Steel Corporation Llanwern		UIC	Union International de Chemins de Fers
BSTE	British Steel Corporation Teeside			
BTP	British Titan Products		(sr)	still running March 1999
GWS	Great Western Society		(sc)	scrapped by March 1999
ICIA	Imperial Chemical Ind. Agricultural Division		(is)	in store March 1999

TOPS codings used in this volume

Code	Wagon Type	Code	Wagon Type
JT	Ironstone tippler, outer, bogie.	PH	Self discharge hopper wagon, 2 axle.
JU	Ironstone tippler, inner, bogie.	PM	Open mineral wagon, 2 axle.
JY	Open aggregate wagon, bogie.	PN	Open aggregate wagon, 2 axle.
KT	Self discharge transfer wagon.	PO	Open steel wagon, 2 axle.
PA	Covered hopper wagon, 2 axle.	PS	Tippler wagon, 2 axle.
PB	Covered hopper wagon, 2 axle.	PT	Pallet van, 2 axle.
PE	Tip Air bulk powder wagon, 2 axle.	PX/JX	Bogie steel wagon.
PG	Hopper wagon, 2 axle.	PR	Mineral wagon, curtain roof, 2 axle.

Brake codings

Follow the above TOPS codings.

Code	Brake type	Code	Brake type
A	Air braked	B	Air braked with through vacuum pipe
F	Vacuum (AFI) braked	G	Vacuum (AFI) braked with through air pipe
O	Unfitted	V	Vacuum braked

Plate 1. P300669 Bolsover. This company operated from collieries at Cresswell, Mansfield, Rufford and Clipstone and had a considerable fleet of wagons from various sources. This one was built by E. Eastgate, Chesterfield in August 1939 and was registered as No. 156277 by the LMS with the company number of B2183. The wooden underframe, with a split in its solebar, is fitted with standard running gear but the original split spoked wheels have been replaced by three hole disc ones. The 7 plank body has side, end and bottom doors and the livery is red oxide with white Gill sans letters, shaded black to the right and below. Other lettering is plain white and corner plates, end and door strapping are black but the diagonal and top one and a half planks of door strapping are red oxide. Ironwork below the solebars is black. All is rather worn and weary and a new top plank has had to be fitted. Photographed in the 1950's.

L.

Plate 2. P112379. Letchworth Electricity Works. Many public utility companies had their own wagons which were used to carry raw materials such as coal. This 13T 8 plank wooden wagon was built to Railway Clearing House standards and has side and end doors, split axleboxes, spindle buffers and runs on three hole disc wheels. Built in July 1936 by the Gloucester Railway Carriage & Wagon Co. Ltd., it carried company No.13 and was registered by the LNER as No. 10007. Livery is red oxide body with white lettering shaded black. Ironwork is black including strapping and end plates, except for the white diagonal and the centre strap on the side door which is red oxide. The company tended to draw its coal from Oxcroft Colliery at Barrow Hill. Photographed in the 1950's.   R.C.

Plate 3. P278600. S.Instone & Co. Ltd. were the principal sales agents for Askern Main Colliery near Doncaster and as such their wagons carried shipping coal to east and west coast ports such as Hull and Preston respectively, as well as ordinary coal products to East Anglia, the Midlands and the South. This all wooden 12T 7 plank wagon has side, end and bottom doors and its tare weight is 6 tons 12cwts. It was built circa. May 1927 by W. Rigley Ltd., Nottingham in a batch numbered 2750-2809. Livery is red oxide with white letters shaded black and all ironwork is black. The lettering is still in good order except for the small italics in white near the tare weight which gave instructions about returning empty to Askern Colliery. Photographed in the 1950's.   L.

Plate 4. P92928. Carlton Collieries Association was the name given in 1927 to the buying and selling agency for a group of collieries originating in 1872 when Carlton Colliery was opened. Wagons travelled widely to the North West, the Midlands and the South. This wagon is a standard 8 plank 13T type with side, end and bottom doors, standard running gear and split spoked wheels. Built by Charles Roberts Ltd. Circa 1927/28 - one of a very large batch - it operated out of Grimethorpe, Frickley or Hatfield Main collieries and the livery is black with white lettering. Photographed in the 1950's. L.

Plate 5. No.1273 Clay Cross Co. Ltd. This is a non-pool standard 7 plank side and end door wagon with a wooden underframe and standard running gear. This company was active in many fields and always advertised its products on the top plank of their wagons, as here, and also on the side doors. No. 1273 has the later style of white lettering on a red oxide body. Photographed in a train on Hatton Bank on 2nd May, 1953. H.F.W./R.C.

Plate 6. P192891. Suncole. This wooden 13T 8 plank wagon is fitted with top rails to give extra volume capacity for the low density 'SUNCOLE/SMOKELESS NOTTINGHAM FUEL' which it carried to consumers in the Midlands and the South. Side, end and bottom doors are fitted and it has standard brakegear and replacement three hole disc wheels. Livery is black overall, 'SUNCOLE' is yellow with vermillion shading and the rays are yellow also. Other lettering is white and that in italics at bottom right originally read - 'Suncole (Nottingham) Ltd./Cinderhill Colliery, Nottingham, LMS', but the tare of 7-1 has painted over some of this. It was built in January 1939 by the L&Y Wagon Works and registered LMS 154777 with company number 5117. These wagons were still running in the late 1950's when this one was photographed. P.J. collection.

Plate 7. P323995. Manners. This colliery was situated at Ilkeston in Derbyshire and this wagon is one of a batch No.1000-1099 built circa. October 1937 by W. Rigley Ltd. of Nottingham. This 13T standard wooden side, end and bottom door wagon is finished in red oxide with white lettering shaded black and has black running gear. Photographed in the 1950's. L.

Plate 8. P117440. The Swansea Navigation Collieries Ltd. This wooden 12T, 7 plank coal wagon has Gloucester Carriage & Wagon Co. Ltd. standard open top axleboxes, stout end posts and the typical spindle buffers. Livery is black overall with white lettering. Founded in 1886, this company finally operated from Mountain Colliery, near Gorseinon which closed in 1969. No. 90618 is one of the Riddles M.O.S. designed 2-8-0 locomotives built in 1943 and purchased by BR in 1948. Its early BR service saw it shedded in the Nottingham / Sheffield area which is when this photograph was taken.   L.

Plate 9. P63984. This 13T 8 plank wooden coal wagon illustrates the annonymous state in which many former private owner wagons eked out their last days on BR. Some were given a coat of light grey paint with white numbers on black patches but this one sports mainly weathered wood, a far cry from the days when it was No.2294 in the fleet of Shelton Iron & Steel Co. and was finished in red oxide with white lettering shaded black. Built in 1934, it was registered as No.128024 by the LMS and was withdrawn in 1962. Photographed at Wadebridge in June 1959.   R.S.

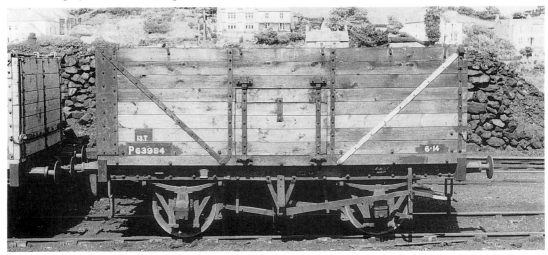

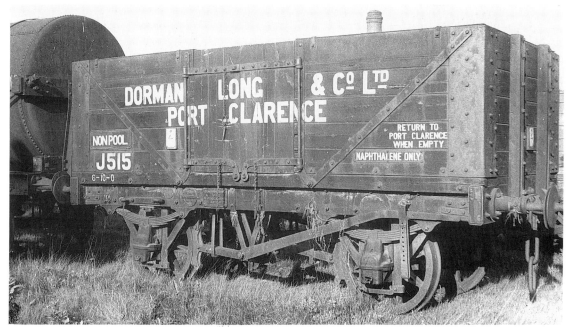

Plate 10. J515. Dorman Long & Co. Ltd. This all wooden mineral wagon was built in 1902 by Hurst Nelson and registered by the North British Railway. The *5* plank body has fixed ends and vertically planked cupboard style doors and its livery is black overall with white lettering. It is dedicated to the conveyance of naphthalene - a white, crystalline, flammable hydrocarbon probably best known for its use in mothballs! Photographed at Port Clarence, Middlesbrough in Summer 1969. D.L.

Plate 11. No.33. The Fife Coal Co. Ltd. became the major producer in the Fife coalfield - Leven being one of its collieries. Large quantities of coal were exported and its products were widely distributed in Scotland. This standard 7 plank 12T wooden wagon was built by the North British Railway and unusually has a four plank side door, as well as two different types of grease axlebox. Note the two door bangers, the commuted charge sign and star to the left of the door. Livery is black with white lettering and white diagonal side strap directed to the open door end of the wagon. The common user policy sees it a long way from its home when it was photographed at Bricket Wood on 14th August, 1948. E.B.

Plate 12. No.1810. Oxcroft Colliery Co. Ltd. near Chesterfield in the East Midlands coalfield exported some coal through Humber ports but mainly produced for the home market. This standard 10T 7 plank wagon has side, end and bottom doors and is fitted with standard running gear. Livery is grey body with white lettering in the reduced economy style. It was built by Charles Roberts & Co. Ltd. and registered by the Lancashire & Yorkshire Railway in 1910. Note the collection of railway-owned horse drays in the background. Photographed at St. Albans City on 23rd May, 1949.   E.B.

Plate 13. T.4. Murgatroyd's. This non-pool 13T 6 plank wooden wagon has semi-rounded ends fitted with brackets to accommodate a sheet rail to cover its load of salt which would normally be carried in containers such as bags or barrels. Built by Charles Roberts & Co. Ltd., it has standard running gear and split spoked wheels. Livery of these wagons was either two shades of grey or yellow and red with white and red lettering. It was photographed in 1959-1960.   L.

Plate 14. No.351. B.Q.C. Ltd. This 10T 3 plank wooden non-pool wagon is typical of the type used to carry processed stone for roadmaking etc. in this case 'For Tarred/Material Only' from 'CEIRIOG/QUARRIES'. In common with some of the preceding wagons, it has different types of axleboxes but typical features include open spoked wheels, round shank spindle buffers and large wooden end posts. Livery is buff coloured body with white lettering shaded black. The small plain white lettering in italic on the right reads 'Empty to/Criggion Quarries/LMR via Shrewsbury'. Photographed at Goodrington Sidings on 8th June, 1957.
R.B.

Plate 15. No.1495 Pilkington Brothers Ltd. This company is one the country's largest manufacturers of glass for which it uses road transported sand from pits at Chelford in Cheshire. This type of tippler wagon was used to carry sand from Chelford and from a railhead at Mill Lane, Rainford to St. Helens when the sand was being carried there from surface deposits on Merseyside. It has many standard constructional features including two-shoe independent brakegear, spindle buffers and runs on split spoked wheels. Note the open front axleboxes. Livery is red body and solebars, white lettering and a white diagonal band edged in black. Corner plates and running gear are black. Photographed in 1964 - these wagons were still in use in 1968.
R.H.

Plate 16. P387394. This 12T *5* plank wooden china clay wagon was built in 1927 and has split axleboxes, spindle buffers, side and end doors and runs on split spoked wheels. Much of its livery is china clay stained wood with white lettering on black patches. Withdrawn in 1959, it was photographed at St. Blazey on 16th June, 1958.

R.S.

Plate 17. No.18. Central Electricity Generating Board. This concern had a large fleet of unfitted 20/21T steel mineral wagons which were used to supply coal to power stations. They were built in 1937 by various builders such as the Metropolitan Carriage & Wagon Co. This wagon shows the typical features with four riveted, side stanchions which extend to the top of the sides, four-shoe brakegear, tie bars, spindle buffers and three hole disc wheels. Livery is grey body with black solebars and below all lettering being white. This one operated to and from Ironbridge Power Station and was photographed at Buildwas in 1961.

P.C.

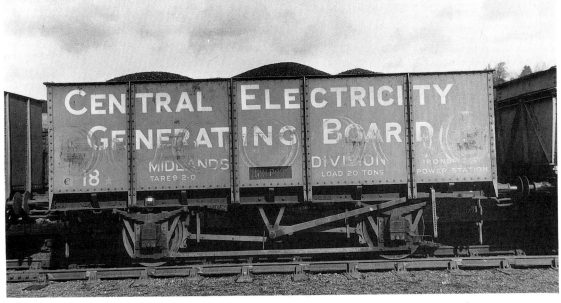

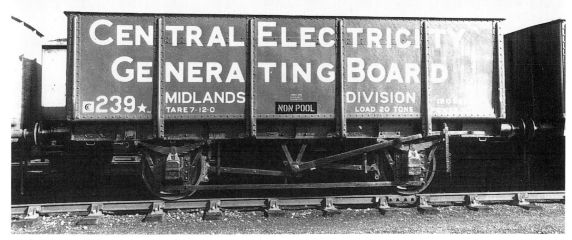

Plate 18. No.239. Central Electricity Generating Board. This wagon is like the one in *plate 17* being 21ft 6ins long with a 12ft 6ins wheelbase but here the six side stanchions are slightly shorter and arranged differently which has led to a different pattern of lettering. Livery is as in *plate 17* but here we see the 'C' mark which is black on a yellow background and shows the company is in the commuted charge scheme paying 1s. per wagon per year rather than paying 1s. per wagon shunting charge and 6d. per wagon per day siding charge. To the right of the number is the yellow star of the 1933 Commuted Empty Haulage Scheme whereby payment of 1d per year allowed for free movement of a defective empty wagon to the repairers. Photographed at Buildwas in 1961. P.C.

Plate 19. No.76. Central Electricity Generating Board. In refurbished condition and now serving the 'MIDLANDS REGION', this wagon has the uneven stanchion pattern seen in *plate 17* and it is designated:- 'To work between/Florence Colliery &/Meaford Power Station'. Note the added strengthening to the ends, side stanchions and the top of the sides. Under TOPS they were coded PMO, but rarely carried it and re-numbered in the 23000-23113 series - the number being applied in white on a black rectangle in the same position as the number here. Photographed at Stoke-on-Trent in 1966. B.H.

Plate 20. P240271. This 21T all steel mineral wagon has riveted construction and side and end doors. It is unfitted with four-shoe brakes and has split axleboxes, tie bars, spindle buffers with ribbed housings and double door bangers for the heavy steel doors. 5,000 of this type were built between 1933 and 1936 by six private builders for the GWR to their diagram N32. These were 'sold' on a 'redemption hire' (hire purchase) basis to 10 different coal distributors, collieries and coal users. The private builders also built these wagons for individual customers. Many were pooled and appeared on BR like this one. Livery is grey with white lettering. Photographed at Bilston West, Hickman's Branch in 1959. P.C.

Plate 21. No.776. I.C.I. This is one of the 16T steel mineral wagons purchased by C.C.Crump from BR and converted in 1971-72 for use by I.C.I's Mond Division to carry soda ash from Northwich to a terminal near Glazebrook on the Manchester Ship Canal where it was end-loaded into ships. Soda ash dissolves and reacts with water to give a corrosive alkaline solution hence the blue sheet and the added roping points on the ends. Some wagons had their side doors removed. The body is blue-green with white lettering, solebars are orange with black lettering and running gear is black. It has two-shoe independent brakegear, spindle buffers, split axleboxes, Instanter couplings and runs on three hole disc wheels. The service finished in 1979 whereupon all the wagons were withdrawn. Photographed at Cadishead in April 1972. D.L.

Plate 22. RLS6305 is the second of the class of PRA/POA 38T gross laden weight (g.l.w.) wagons built by Standard Wagon in 1983, in this case to design code PO 023A. The class numbered 6304-6316 and they were built using the underframes from redundant APCM palvans, in this case APCM 6240. Note how the body is shorter than the underframes and how mechanical unloading has bowed the sides. It has Oleo buffers, roller bearings, eight-shoe clasp style air brakes, a long handbrake lever and double link suspension. Livery is mostly weathered rust with black lettering on a white square. This type was used to carry agricultural lime to Scotland and scrap metal in the North East of England but they were redundant by 1987 and were stored at Goole which is where this one was photographed on 7th February, 1993 (sc).

S.J.

Plate 23. RLS6307. TOPS coded PRA, this clay hood is in the same class as No.6305 in *plate 22* and had the same origin but it has end platforms served by ladders and the shape of the body ends are different to allow for the fitting of a roller hood to keep the china clay dry. The underframe details are as in *plate 22* except for the double link 14 leaf spring suspension here. Livery is weathered and corroded grey with black lettering on a white square. Solebars and below are black and the hood is red. Photographed at Carlisle *en* route from Ponts Mill to Scotland on 26th August ,1986 (sc). A.T.

Plate 24. RLS6325 is the last of the second class of 36T (g.l.w.) mineral wagons, (6317-6325), which were built by Standard Wagon also using the 16ft wheelbase underframes from redundant APCM palvans. Of the three batches built, this one had lower and longer bodies which like the solebars and below here are finished in rusting light grey with white lettering on black and black lettering on the body colour. They were used for the same purposes as RLS 6305 in *plate 22* but were redundant by 1987 and scrapped in 1992. Photographed at Leicester on 28th May, 1988.   A.T.

Plate 25. TRL5151. TOPS coded POA, this 46T (g.l.w.) open wagon is the last of 10, which were built by grafting a new body onto a former ferry tank wagon underframe, (from 707499311-2 in this case), where the original brake platform has been retained. They were built by C.C.Crump in 1985 to design code PO 015A and the length over buffers is 35ft. Note the U.I.C. double link suspension and buffers and the short handbrake lever. Livery is light grey with black lettering and running gear. They were variously hired to carry china clay, processed kelp, lime and baled scrap but were scrapped by 1995. Photographed at Southall in November 1987.   B.D.

Plate 26. TRL5187 is from the class of 46T (g.l.w.) open wagons numbered 5182 to 5193 which were converted under design code PO 017A using former tank wagon (TTA) underframes - in this case TRL 51943 - by C.C.Crump in 1987. They are 35ft long and have FAT 28 parabolic single link suspension and robust U.I.C. Ferry-style buffers. Livery is weathered light grey body with black lettering on white patches and black running gear. Foster Yeoman used them from Merehead and English China Clays carried china clay in them from Drinnick Mill to Scotland. Scrapped by 1995. Photographed at Padiham Power Station on 7th December, 1991.

S.J.

Plate 27. TRL 5463. TOPS coded POA, this 33.5T (load) open wagon of design code PN 016N has a tare weight of 12.2T and comes from the class numbered 5457-5489 which have the same origins as TRL 5187, (TRL 51601 in this case) emerging from C.C.Crump's in 1988. Livery is similar also but note how the body sides have different strengthening arrangements. Access ladders are provided at diagonally opposite corners. Only 5467 was left (in store) by 1995. Photographed at St. Blazey on 24th June, 1992.

A.T

Plate 28. TRL 5402 was produced to design code PN 016K in a similar way to 5463 using the underframe from former TTA tank wagon TRL 51816 and we see here the other side of the brakegear. End and side strengthening is the same as in *plate 27* but the light grey body carries the blue Yeoman 'Y' on a white panel here; solebars and below are black. The first of the class, (5402-5416), it was photographed at Gwaun-cae-Gurwen on 24th October, 1992 when working from Merehead but by 1995 it had been scrapped.

S.J.

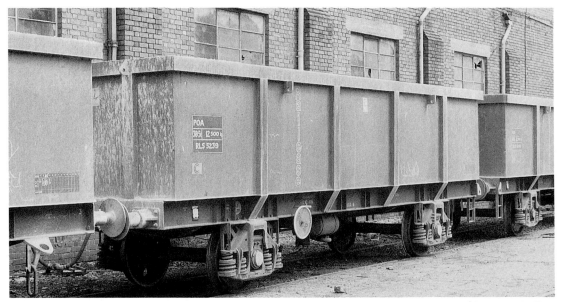

Plate 29. RLS5239. This class of 51T (g.l.w.), 32ft long POA open wagons, (5234-5253), were built to design code PO 018B by Standard Wagon in 1987 using former bulk tippler (PEA) underframes, (RLS 12239 in this case). Note side and end lifting lugs, a handbrake operating wheel and BSC Friction Pedestal suspension. Livery is grey with a black TOPS panel lettered in white and the vertical 'Railease' lettering is light blue edged in white. By 1995 those left were in internal use at Halewood. Photographed at Sheffield Darnall on 20th May, 1989.   A.T.

Plate 30. PDUF4535. TOPS coded POA, this is one of the 60 open scrap wagons (4500-4559) built by Powell Duffryn, Cardiff in 1988-89, in this case to design code PO 016V. All utilised redundant TTA underframes, in this case former bitumen tank SUKO61725 which was originally built by Powell Duffryn in 1967. It has plain plate axleguards with roller bearings and double link suspension with parabolic springs. Ladders are provided at the lefthand end of each side and note the hinged, cupboard-style inspection hatch which opens outwards. Wheelbase is 16ft and it measures 28ft 11ins over buffers. Livery is weathered black overall with white lettering, the 'SS' logo being red and blue edged in white as seen in *plate 48*. Photographed at Oxford Station in Spring 1991. In use at Allied Steel & Wire, Cardiff as KW937, March 1999.   B.D.

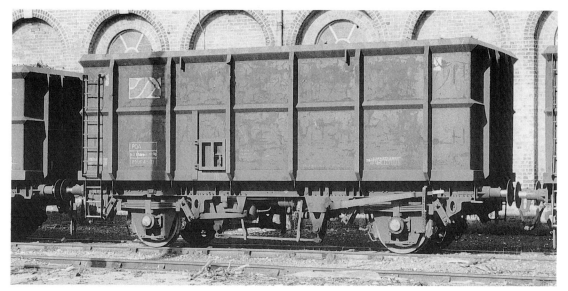

Plate 31. PDUF4581 has a similar style of body to the wagon in *plate 30* but it was constructed in 1989 by Powell Duffryn to design code PO 021A using the underframes from 'Presflo' wagon APCM 9021. It is only 27ft 1ins. long but has a taller body giving it a similar (g.l.w.) to PDUF 4535 with which it shares a common livery. Note the single link parabolic spring suspension and the complex handbrake linkages to the eight-shoe clasp style air brakes. On hire to Allied Steel Wales working to and from the plant at Cardiff, it was photographed at Exeter Riverside on 20th June, 1992 (sr).   A.T.

Plate 32. RLS5900 is the prototype/demonstrator 51T g.l.w. scrap carrier built to design code PO 010A, (BR diagram 6/539), by Standard Wagon, Heywood and intended for sale or hire through its Railease subsidiary. After trials it was modified by removal of the top lip of the body and the single side door/inspection hatch was converted to bottom hinging as seen here. Ladders on diagonal end corners give top access for inspection of the load or the interior. The channel underframe has Oleo pneumatic buffers, and English Steel Corporation Friction Pedestal suspension. Livery is yellow body with black lettering and underframe. A drawing appeared on *page 531* of 'Model Railway Constructor' October 1986. Photographed at Milton Park, Abingdon on 18th June, 1981.   B.D.

Plate 33. RLS5911 is in the same class of 20, (5900-5919), as 5900 in the previous plate but was built to design code PO 010B by Standard Wagon in 1982, being 26ft 1ins over headstocks with a wheelbase of 16ft, increases of 1ft 9ins and 1ft respectively on the dimensions of the prototype. End and side bracing have been changed to give more support and there are lifting lugs. Note the absence of ladders and the use of Gloucester Floating axle suspension. Livery is very weathered blue sides and yellow ends with scarcely visible white lettering. All were scrapped by 1992. Photographed at Bescot on 9th October, 1988.

A.T.

Plate 34. RLS5085 seen in the foreground here is one of the 100 (5000-5099) 51T g.l.w. POA open scrap carriers built by Standard Wagon in 1984 to design code PO 014A. These were rebuilds of the PG 014A BSC Ravenscraig hopper wagons the body being mounted on the strengthened and extended underframe whilst the running gear was retained. It is 29ft 6½ins long with a wheelbase of 16ft. The body has considerable strengthening and there are access/inspection ladders on diagonally opposite corners which have internal footsteps in the corner plating. Note how the robust end capping has been broken off and the angled top plates to the side strengtheners to prevent dust and swarf settling when loading. Livery is as in *plate 33*. Photographed at Tinsley, Sheffield on 26th March, 1988,but gone by 1995. A.T.

Plate 35. RLS5225 was converted from the PEA tippler wagon RLS12225 by Standard Wagon in 1987. 20 wagons were produced (5214-5233), which were hired for scrap carrying, for example by Allied Steel Wales in 1992. Livery is as in *plate 48*, Railease being in blue edged in white. Note the white handbrake control wheel, BSC Friction Pedestal suspension and the general lack of underframe detail. Photographed at Sheffield Darnall on 17th December, 1988 (sr). A.T.

Plate 36. BSCO20123 and 20041 are two of the 700 16T steel bodied tippler wagons built in 1939-1940 by Charles Roberts & Co. Ltd. for Stewarts and Lloyds to carry home-produced iron ore to their blast furnaces at Corby. They were taken over by BSC on nationalisation and lasted until circa. 1978 when home ore production ceased. Each wagon has one axle of spoked and one of disc wheels as well as two-shoe one sided brake gear (operable from both sides). Livery is grey body with black running gear and white lettering. TOPS coding was PSO but is not shown here when the wagons were photographed at Toton in September 1978. D.L.

Plate 37. BTP24398 is one of the batch of tippler wagons No.24301-24600 rebuilt from 1974-1978 by W.H.Davis of Langwith Junction for British Titan Products using shortened redundant 35T class B tank wagon underframes. Built to design code PS 015A, this one has red capping to its light grey body underframes and running gear being black. The company name is in blue but other lettering is white and that on the central panel reads 'TO WORK BETWEEN/IMMINGHAM DOCKS/AND GRIMSBY ONLY'. Note the eight-shoe clasp brakes, Skefco roller bearings, Oleo buffers and Instanter couplings. Tare is 9.75Tand load 25.5T. Photographed at Immingham on 17th July ,1992 but gone by 1995.   A.T.

Plate 38. BTP24306 is from the same batch of wagons as seen in the above plate but it was built to the alternative design code PS 005A. Note one split and one open front axlebox per side and spindle buffers. It has a tare weight of 8.94T and load of 21.1T and the capping to its light grey body is yellow. Other livery details are as for 24398 above. Photographed at Immingham on 16th August, 1992.   S.J.

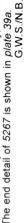

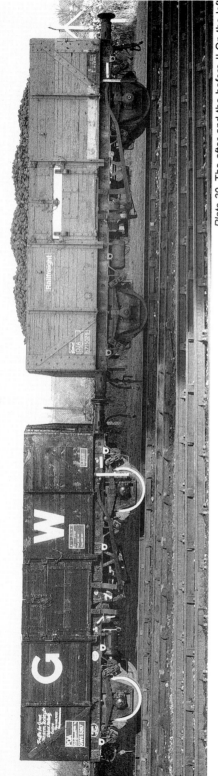

Plate 39. The after and the before !! On the left is GWS 5267, a POA class open wagon which was built by BR at Lancing works in 1957 to diagram 1/055, lot 2851, (20 wagons, B715020-715039). It was originally B715024 and it still carries this wagon plate on the solebar above the lefthand spring hanger. As a 21T general goods wagon, it had a sheet support rail and was designed for Continental traffic hence the U.I.C. pattern buffers and double link suspension. It also has plate axleguards, roller bearings, eight-shoe style clasp brakes and lifting lugs. Transfer to private ownership took place in 1989 and it carries locomotive coal for use at Didcot Railway Centre. Length is 27ft, load 21.5T and tare weight 11.45T. Livery is dark (G.W.) grey with white lettering, that at the top left in italic reads:- 'Traffic for Great/Western Society Ltd./ Didcot Railway Centre/Tops code 74311Telephone (0235) 81720'. On the right is the other wagon of this type owned by G.W.S. Didcot Ltd. still carrying its original Railfreight livery and BR numbering B715029. Now numbered GWS 5268, it has the same livery as 5267 in this photograph which was taken at Didcot Railway Centre on 14th January, 1989. The end detail of 5267 is shown in *plate 39a*.

G.W.S./N.B.

Plate 39a.

Plate 40. BSCO 25197 is one of the batch of 27.5T unfitted ironstone hoppers which were re-bodied by W.H. Davis in 1973 from the original 16.5T sloping sided wagons built for Stewarts & Lloyds in 1939-40 by Charles Roberts & Co. Ltd. *(see plate 36 for similar wagons)*. Note the long white handbrake lever, four-shoe brakes, open front axleboxes, spindle buffers and Instanter couplings. Body is light grey with rust patches and apart from a white number on a black patch, the lettering is black. Solebars and below are rusty black. These wagons were redundant when British iron ore production ceased in 1977-78 but this one escaped to Cottesmore where it was photographed in original condition on 25th May, 1991.   A.T.

Plate 41. PR25509. TOPS coded PSA this 45T g.l.w. mineral tippler wagon is one of 24, (25500-25523), which were built by Procor in 1975 to design codes PS016B and PS016C - the former in this case, using redundant tank wagon underframes which were fitted with air brakes. Wheelbase is 15ft and with a load of 33.25T the tare weight here is 12.5T. Double link parabolic taper leaf spring suspension is fitted here and it retains the hand brakegear of the original tank wagon. Livery is rusty light grey with many patches of fresh grey paint and white lettering on black or vice versa except for 'caib' which is red. Various companies hired them including Capper Pass, I.C.I., Steetley Minerals and Tilling Construction for the movement of limestone, salt and agricultural lime but by 1992 they were stored at Peak Forest which is where this one was photographed on 17th December,1989. By 1995 they were no longer extant.   A.T

Plate 42. PR3000 - the only one of its kind, this bogie box wagon was built to design code JX 030C by Procor in 1974. TOPS coded PXA, tare weight is 32.4T, load 69.9T and length over buffers is 55ft. It is lower in height than the others in this class *(see plate 43),* but like them it is used to carry scrap steel to Sheerness from various scrapyards. Note the heavy duty buffers and the Gloucester MkII clasp bogies. Livery is light blue body, dark blue underframe and black bogies, all lettering being white. Photographed at Ridham Dock on 7th June, 1992 (sr). A.T.

Plate 43. PR3001 - also built in 1974 by Procor but this wagon shows the typical features of the class being of design code JX 030B. Underframe details are as for PR 3000 and the livery is also the same, differences appear in the greater height of the body and ends here which results in the slight changes in external bracing. Photographed at Ridham Dock on 7th June, 1992 (sr). A.T.

Plate 44. PR3121 is one of 30 out of the class ot 40 bogie box wagons which were built to design code JX 029A by Procor in 1982-83 (Class numbers were 3100 -3139) 3130 to 3139 were built to design code JX 029B. All were hired to Sheerness Steel initially but by 1995 some were in use elsewhere and some were in store. Length is 62ft 7ins and it is fitted with Schlieren M25 bogies set at 37ft 8¾ins centres. The solebars are like extensions of the reinforced body which has a small door at the righthand end of each side for cleaning and access purposes - since the hand rungs on the ends are invariably damaged as here. Note the scrap deflector plate which was fitted to the ends of the first 30 vehicles. Livery is similar to that in *plates 42 and 43* albeit rather more 'weary'. Photographed at Oxford in December 1986 (sr).   B.D.

Plate 45. OK3279 is one of the outer wagons from the single class of 102T g.l.w. bogie box wagons, (3268-3328), which were built in 1988 by Orenstein & Koppel, Dortmund, Germany. Outer wagons had robust buffers with square heads at one end and drawgear so they could be coupled to a locomotive or a different type of wagon - the other end has a fixed bar type of coupling to the next wagon in the rake. Measuring 42ft 1ins, in length with a wheelbase of 18ft 10ins, it has a heavily reinforced body with a full height door at the lefthand end of each side and it runs on O&K type 25-100 bogies which have double link suspension to each wheel. Livery is as for 3321 in *plate 47* albeit rather more weathered with almost whitewashed out Yeoman boards. Photographed at Stratford on 29th July,1994 (sr).   A.T.

Plate 46. PLAS5438. This 37ft. long open wagon has fixed steel plate ends but the sides are flimsy collapsible lattice panels. Built to design code PN 019A in 1988 by W.H.Davis of Langwith Junction, it is one of the class of 30 (5417-5446), which used former BR VCA and ZRA van underframes, (in this case ADC200426). The wheelbase is 20ft 9ins and this class is dedicated to running the Plasmor building block service from Great Heck near Doncaster. Seen here at Whitemoor on 3rd September, 1989 (sr).   A.T.

Plate 47. OK3321 is an inner wagon in the same class as No. 3279 in *plate 45* TOPS coded PHA, it has the same build details as seen in 3279 but being an inner rake wagon, it has fixed couplings at each end. Operation is in aggregate trains from Merehead and this one was photographed at Banbury in April 1989 (sr).   B.D.

Plate 48. RLS4605 built to design code PO 022A by Standard Wagon in 1989, this 30.5T POA scrap steel wagon is the penultimate one in the class, (4596-4606). These wagons had new bodies grafted onto redundant 16ft wheelbase PMA underframes - RLS6326 in this case and it was photographed ex-works at Heywood on 12th July, 1989. Hired to Allied Steel Wales it operates from the Cardiff works (sr).   A.T.

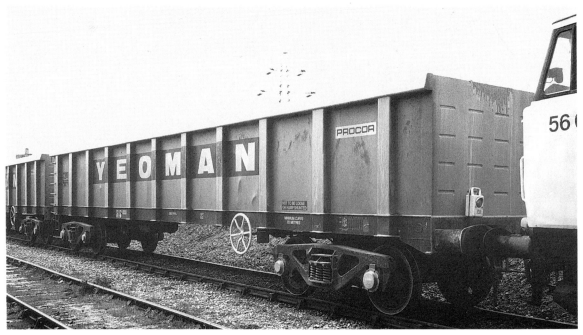

Plate 49. PR3162. TOPS coded PXA, this is one of the four outer bogie box wagons from the class 3100-3169 which were numbered 3160-63 and were built by Procor in 1987 to design code JN 029F (inners were to E). Note the very large white spoked handbrake wheel, heavy duty buffers and Gloucester 3 piece cast steel bogies with roller bearings. Operating like the O&K wagons, it has a similar livery except for no 'Y' panel and it has blue solebars and bogies. Photographed at Banbury in April 1989 (sr). B.D.

Plate 50. PR3240 is one of the class of 78, (3170-3247), 102T g.l.w. bogie box wagons of design code KE 029G (in this case) which were built by Procor in 1987-88. Note the end inspection platform, the Association of American Railroads type auto coupling and Gloucester 3 piece cast steel bogies. The livery is that carried when it was used by Trans-Manche Link in connection with the work on the Channel Tunnel, *see plate 53*. These wagons were still operational in 1995 working Reading West/Stoke Gifford aggregate trains. Photographed at Swindon on 1st May, (sr). T.R.

Plate 51. PR5310 is one of the class of 12, (5300-5311), 70T g.l.w. bogie open pallet wagons built in 1977-78 by Procor to design code JO 001B and hired to ICI Mond for transporting small quantities of special chemicals such as chlorine, from Runcorn to Willesden. In 1986 they were modified to run as seen here carrying roofing tiles for Redland. 63ft 7ins long, it runs on Gloucester Fastfreight bogies set at 42ft centres. Note the sturdy steel fixed ends and five wooden planked dropside doors with controllers. Livery is as seen in *plate 55.* Most were in store in 1992 but by 1995 they were in internal use at Scunthorpe Steel. Photographed at Norwich on 30th May, 1987. A.T.

Plate 52. REDA92641 started life as one of the last batch of Railease bogie flats which were built in 1988 to design code KF 010A by Standard Wagon and used on trial by Freightliners Ltd. for a year after which they were converted by the builders for use by Redland to carry roofing tiles. The sides here are dropside steel panel doors with controllers. Livery is as in *plate 55,* length being 67ft 4ins and g.l.w. 81.95T. Sambre et Meuse VNH 1 bogies are fitted. By 1992 all were in store but they were later given some use by Tioxide UK Ltd. at Grimsby before being in store again by 1995. Photographed at Bank Quay Station, Warrington on 16th August, 1989. A.T.

Plate 53. PR3201. TOPS coded PXA, is a 102T g.l.w. bogie box wagon from the same class as 3240 in *plate 50* but it is an outer vehicle built to design code KE 02911 and has buffers at the far end. Photographed at Hoo Junction on 7th June, 1992, it carries the TML livery and logo relating to its work on the Channel Tunnel contract (sr).   A.T.

Plate 54. PR14466 is the last of the class of 33, 51T g.l.w. PGA open aggregate hoppers built to design code PG 013E by Procor in 1981. This was the last class of four wheel aggregate hoppers built for hire to Foster Yeoman. It has deep channel solebars, parallel buffers and Gloucester floating axle suspension. Note how the brake pipes run through the bottom of the four

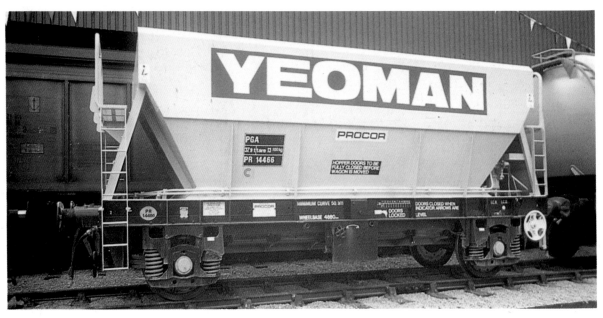

hopper side stays. Still operating in 1995, it was photographed on 18th June, 1981 at Milton Park, Abingdon, Oxon (sr).   B.D.

Plate 55. REDA14816. This 51T g.l.w. PGA aggregate hopper is one of the class of 40, (14800-14839), built to design code PG 012A by Standard Wagon in 1978 for Redland Aggregates. The 16ft wheelbase chassis is 22ft 3ins long and has central solebar-mounted hopper control gear, short handbrake levers and Gloucester floating axle suspension. Still active in 1995, it had worked continuously from Mountsorrel and was photographed at Didcot in June 1987 (sr).   B.D.

Plate 56. PR8251 was built in 1971 by Standard Wagon to design code PG 002D. The class of 50, (8204-8253), 46T g.l.w. open salt hoppers were initially hired by BP Chemicals but they moved on to other loads such as alumina between Hull and Stafford. By 1995 they were stored at Hindlow. Photographed at March on 3rd September, 1989 (is).   A.T.

Plate 57. BSSW26651 is one of the class of 114, (26564-26677), 102T g.l.w. bogie tipplers - in this case an inner wagon of design code JU 003A. Constructed by Redpath, Dorman Long, Middlesbrough in 1974, they are dedicated to the movement of ironstone between Port Talbot and Llanwern.

Special rotary automatic couplings are fitted at the orange painted ends of these wagons. Photographed at Cardiff Central Station on 12th October, 1988 (sr).   B.D.

Plate 58. TCS14405 is one of the 33, (14400-14432) 51T g.l.w. hoppers built by BREL Shildon in 1975 to design code PG 008A. They were used to carry crushed limestone between Swinden and either Hull or Leeds but by 1995 they were in storage. Top loading was by conveyor and bottom discharge was pneumatically operated. Note the characteristic shape of the hopper and the BSC Friction Pedestal suspension. Photographed at Hull on 30th March, 1992 (is).   S.J.

Plate 59. BSSC 26102 was built by BREL Shildon in 1972 for British Steel to carry imported iron ore from Immingham Docks to Scunthorpe. It is a 102T g.l.w. bogie tippler wagon of the class 26000-26106 and is an outer vehicle built to design code JT 001C having Oleo buffers and a screw coupling at one end and an auto coupling at the other. The design of the reinforcing stays is different to other wagons of the type and these are the only ones to run on FBT bogies which are set at 23ft centres, length being 41ft. Ends and first side panel are freshly painted light grey with white lettering the rest of the side is dirty rusty coloured and the bogies are black. Photographed at Immingham on 16th April, 1989 (sc).   A.T.

Plate 60. BSSW 26675. TOPS coded JTA, this bogie tippler is from the same class as No. 26651 in *plate 57* but it is an outer wagon to design code JT 003C and has buffers and a screw coupling at one end as seen here. These 1974-built tipplers all run on BSC Axle Motion bogies. Note the horizontal reinforcements on the end and the freshly painted Rail Blue patches with white lettering on an otherwise faded blue body. Photographed at Cardiff Central Station on 26th September, 1997 (sr).   T.R.

Plate 61. PR26512 built by Redpath, Dorman Long, Middlesbrough in 1972 to design code JU 002D - an inner rake tippler which was originally used to carry iron ore to Consett Steelworks. Note the similarity between this wagon and No. 26675 in the previous plate. Purchased and overhauled by Procor, it is here on hire to Foster Yeoman operating out of Merehead. Livery is as seen on the back cover and it was photographed at Westbury on 10th August ,1991.   S.J.

Plate 62. PR26817 was originally BSTE26507 built by Redpath, Dorman Long in 1972-73. Now in ARC service this inner vehicle has had its couplings fixed and it is TOPS coded JUA. Livery is as in *plate 64* - the bogie side frames being the same colour as the large ARC letters. Photographed at Newport Alexandra Dock Junction on 26th September, 1997 (sc).   S.J.

Plate 63. RLS14705. TOPS coded PGA, this is the 38.5T g.l.w. prototype for the Tarmac Roadstone hoppers TAMC 14900-14921 which operated from Topley Pike. It was built by Standard Wagon in 1977 and measures 21ft 7ins in length with a wheelbase of 15ft. Unique features are a single set of hopper doors and very basic end ladders and platform. Stored at Taunton by 1995. Photographed at Milton Park, Abingdon on 18th June 1981(sc).   B.D.

Plate 64. PR14688 is the first of the small class of 17 (14688-14704), 51T g.l.w. aggregate hoppers to design code PG 006B built by Standard

Wagon in 1975. Note the deep flat sided solebar sloping down at the ends, protective end plates, loops on the hopper top and side and end cleats for roping a sheet. Photographed in store at Taunton on 19th June, 1992 but back in operation in 1995 (sc).   A.T.

Plate 65. BIS7834. This 51T g.l.w. covered hopper was one of 20 (7825-7844) built to design code PA 0012B by Standard Wagon in 1983. Used to transport sand from Middleton Towers to Cudworth. Photographed at March on 3rd September, 1989 (sr).   A.T.

Plate 66. THOM28001 is one of the five (28000-28004) 88T g.l.w. bogie side tippler wagons built to design code JQ 005A by Standard Wagon in 1985 for W & M Thompson to carry agricultural mag-lime between Ferryhill and Montrose from where it is distributed by Scottish hauliers Carnegie. Two side-tipping boxes are carried on a 45ft 11ins long underframe mounted on Sambre et Meuse Y25C bogies set at 31ft centres. Livery is dark grey with white lettering. Photographed at Montrose on 17th August, 1987 (is).   A.T.

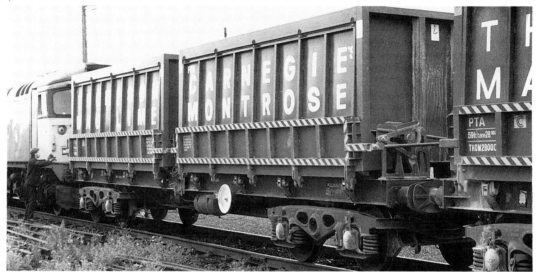

Plate 67. Taken on the same occasion as *plate 66*, this shows one of the boxes of THOM28001 being unloaded and the hydraulic rams can be seen. Note the prominent white handbrake control wheels.   A.T.

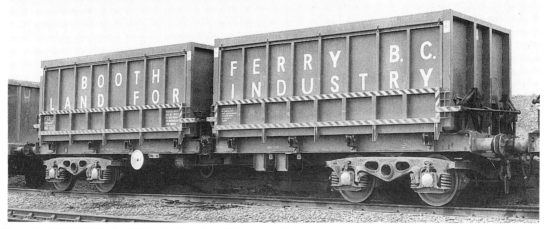

Plate 68. BBC28009. In 1986-88 Standard Wagon built four more of the bogie side tipplers, given design code JQ 005B and numbered 28009-12 on similar underframes to the Thompson wagons but having a tare of 27.5T and g.l.w. of 90T compared to 28T and 88T respectively for the former wagons. Livery is similar but these wagons, owned by Boothferry Borough Council, were used to carry spoil from Hatfield Colliery to a landfill site at Glews Hollow, Goole. By 1992 they were in store at Goole; the new owners Caib hired them to Mendip Rail to work from Whatley.
Photographed at Goole on 25th March, 1990 (is).   A.T.

Plate 69. No.3 Robert Hutchison & Co. Ltd. is an early type of grain hopper with a wooden body and underframe. It has two-shoe independent brakegear, short shank spindle buffers and split spoked wheels. Loading is via the hatches in the roof which have hinged covers. Note the massive timber end posts, large corner plates and delicate side strapping. Livery is red oxide with white lettering shaded black and black ironwork. Photographed at Kirkcaldy Harbour on 18th June, 1965.   R.C.

Plate 70. No.6 Robert Hutchison & Co. Ltd. Photographed in company with No.3 in the above plate, this grain hopper shares many common features with the latter but its livery has faded and former ownership can be detected by the large letters LGW, Leith General Warehousing, another Scottish carrier whose grain wagons had the same livery as its new owner. Subtle differences here include corner strengthening plates and no central vertical side strapping.   R.C.

Plate 71. No.48 S.G.D. Scottish Grain Distillers had a fleet of these 20T hoppers which were built to LMS Diagram D1689 by Hurst Nelson in 1937. Note the tie bars, three hole disc wheels and the short handbrake lever operating two-shoes on the outside of the wheels via the cross shaft. The handwheel controls the bottom discharge and the step to its left and the side trapdoor are on this side only. Wheelbase is 10ft 6ins and length over headstocks is 21ft 6ins. Used to carry barley malt from Scottish sources to Windygates, they were withdrawn in 1981. Livery detail is seen in the picture on the rear cover. Photographed at Cameron Bridge in Summer 1970. D.L.

Plate 72. BCH7803 - Bass, Charrington No.3 is one of the first 12 of the 24 of these 31T g.l.w. hoppers, (7801-7812) which were built to BR diagram 1/270. Note the mix of split and open front axleboxes, two bottom discharge hopper control wheels, outer brake shoes only and riveted construction. Livery is red body with white lettering and black solebars and below. These wagons were transferred to private ownership in 1967 and carried barley malt from East Anglia to Burton-on-Trent until replaced by road transport in the 1970's. Photographed at Burton-on-Trent in Spring 1975. D.L.

Plate 73. BCH7815 - Bass, Charrington No.15 is one of the later group of grain hoppers, (7813-7824) built to BR diagram 1/271. The side stays are not carried over the roof and there are full length catwalks on both sides of the two sliding roof hatches. Note the all-welded construction here. Livery is as in *plate 72* and it was photographed on the same occasion.   D.L.

Plate 74. BRT5894. The Maltsters Association of Great Britain entered into a contract with BR in 1966 to carry barley malt from the Eastern Counties to a railhead at Dufftown in Scotland. This wagon was the first of the batch of 35 hired from BRTE and it was one of the sequence 5810-5924 built to design code PA 003A in 1965-66 by Routes Pressings. Livery is yellow overall with white boards carrying black lettering. The wagon is rather grimy and the BRTE board cannot be read. It has the special linked vacuum brake gear, (to avoid the bottom discharge hopper), Oleo hydraulic buffers, roller bearings and double link spring suspension. One of the vacuum cylinders is visible on the left. Photographed at Doncaster in Summer 1969.   D.L.

Plate 75. BRT6050 is one of the second batch of bulk grain hoppers, 6025-6054, built to design code PA 003B by Powell Duffryn in 1966. The end ladders lead to catwalks giving access to the four top loading hatches. The wheelbase is 15ft and length is 29ft 1in. Like No. 5894 in *plate 74*, it is a Maltsters Association wagon but the side boards are orange with white lettering whilst the BRT board has 'B' and 'T' in white on red and 'R' is white on black. Photographed at Doncaster in Summer 1969.   D.L.

Plate 76. BRT6143 is one of the third batch of grain hoppers, (6055-6154) which were built to design code PA 004A by Powell Duffryn in 1967-68. The hopper body here only has five side stanchions, the side boards are smaller and square in shape, (some like these were also fitted to some of the earlier wagons however), and the double link spring suspension has 11 leaves instead of 7. There is no BRT plate here and the vacuum cylinder can therefore be seen. Livery is blue overall which led to the wagons being called 'Blues'. Photographed at Doncaster in Summer 1969.   D.L.

Plate 77. BRT7640 is from the same batch as 6050 in *plate 75* but it has been refurbished and the side boards and their fixings have been removed and it has the stronger 11 leaf spring suspension. TOPS code is PAV carried on the white panel. Photographed at Didcot in November 1979.   B.D.

Plate 78. BRT7755 is from the same batch of Grainflow 'minbulks' as No. 7745 seen on the front cover picture but we see the other side of the brakegear here. Both have the same build details but this one was converted to design code PA 004D and is TOPS coded PAB. Only 10 were still carrying grain by 1988 and by 1992 all 35 left were in store of which 7 remained in 1995 - 5 stored at Thornton Junction and one each at Immingham and Healey Mills. Photographed at March on 7th April, 1991.   A.T.

Plate 79. PR8018 is one of the class of 50 (8000-8049), 45T g.l.w. covered hoppers built by Standard Wagon in 1970-71 for hire via Procor (UK) Ltd. to carry lime, which is top loaded and bottom discharged through two hoppers. It has a wheelbase of 16ft and is 30ft long. Note the double link suspension, Oleo hydraulic buffers and unusual handbrake linkages. The characteristically shaped body is covered in lime and only part of the Procor logo is visible. In 1992, those left were operated by Steetley Minerals between Thrislington and Hartlepool but all had gone by 1995. Photographed at Grassington in Summer 1973. D.L.

Plate 80. PR8004. TOPS coded PAA, this hopper has the same build details as No.8001 in *plate 79* but we see the opposite side here. This is one of the batch which were modified to carry alumina by fitting four circular fillers on the hopper top instead of the three hinged hatches. The hopper body is dark brown and the solebars are freshly painted in light grey. All lettering is white, (except for Procor which appears black). Photographed at Tees Yard on 2nd June, 1990. A.T.

Plate 81. BRT8060 is one of the 69 (8050-8118) 45T g.l.w. covered hoppers built in 1972-73 by Standard Wagon for British Railway Traffic & Electric Co. These wagons have the same design features as the Procor batch *(see plates 79 and 80)* except for BSC Friction Pedestal suspension, handbrake wheels and no through vacuum pipe. Layers of lime have obliterated the hopper colouring and such lettering as can be seen is mainly white. The batch was on long term hire to British Steel Teeside carrying lime from Shap Quarry for use in the blast furnaces at Lackenby and Redcar but by 1995 only one remained - 8088, which was in store at Thornaby. Photographed at Shap on 28th August, 1991.   A.T.

Plate 82. BSGL8190. Built to design code PB 008A by BREL Ashford in 1974-75 for the British Steel Corporation, this is one of the class of 50 covered hoppers (8150-8199) used to carry lime from Shap to the steelmaking plant at Ravenscraig near Motherwell. There are six side stays to the body which has a full length top hatch with cover and two bottom discharge hoppers. It has a wheelbase of 20ft 3ins and is 30ft 3½ins long over the Oleo pneumatic buffers. Note the BSC Friction Pedestal suspension and air brakes with a wheel control handbrake. The livery is not visible here due to an overall surface coating of lime which has obliterated all lettering. Photographed at Shap on 28th August,1991 (sr).   A.T.

Plate 83. BRT12101 is the second of the class of 17, 46T g.l.w. covered hoppers built to design code PA 007A in 1971 by Standard Wagon. TOPS coded PAA but not carried here, these wagons were in use by Anglesey Aluminium to transport petroleum coke from Immingham to Holyhead when this one was photographed at Immingham on 17th July, 1992. Loading is via four top hatches and there are two bottom discharge hoppers. Wheelbase is 20ft 3ins and length 33ft 9ins and it is fitted with Gloucester Friction Pedestal suspension. Note the shape of the hopper body which aids the settling of the petroleum coke. Livery is weathered brown with white lettering on black patches, the logo being blue and red on a white background (sr). A.T.

Plate 84. ALCN12020. In 1971 BREL Ashford built 19 of these 32T covered hoppers (12017-12035) to design code PA 006A for Alcan to transport imported alumina (aluminium oxide) from Blyth Docks to their factory at Lynemouth, and they could also be used to carry petroleum coke. TOPS coded PAO, the design was based on the earlier BR Covhop. BR Friction Link suspension was fitted but there was no continuous braking as they were restricted to 45mph and only travelled over freight only lines. Livery is grey body with black lettering and a small blue Alcan logo. They were still operating in 1992 but had gone by 1995. Photographed at Blyth on 2nd September, 1989. A.T.

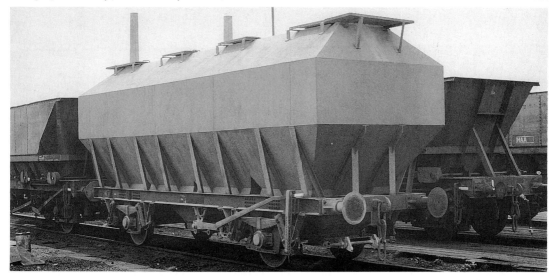

Plate 85. TRL12804 is one of the class of 8 (12000-12007) 51T g.l.w. covered hoppers of TOPS code PAA which were built by Standard Wagon in 1982 to design code PA 010A and hired to Tullis Russell by Tiger Rail Ltd. They are 26ft long with a wheelbase of 16ft and were used to convey china clay from Cornwall to the Tullis Russell paper mill at Markinch. By 1995 they were in store at Mossend yard. Two handwheels control the bottom discharge and there is a small handbrake lever. Note the channel solebars, Oleo buffers and Gloucester Floating axle suspension. Livery is dark blue with black underframe - heavily coated with china clay here, 'Tullis Russell The Papermakers' is in blue on a white background and the TRL logo is black and maroon on a yellow panel with black lettering. Photographed at St. Blazey on 24th June, 1992 (sc).   A.T.

Plate 86. PR14153/2/4/5 - the entire class of 51T g.l.w. hoppers built by Procor in 1975 to design code PB 009A which were fitted with covers when hired for grain traffic on the Derwent Valley Railway. There are three sets of bottom discharge doors and the end ladders (diagonally arranged on opposite ends) give top access. Livery is featured on the back cover.

Photographed at Middlesbrough on 1st September, 1989 (is).   A.T.

Plate 87. ICIA14175 built to design code PA 009B by Procor in 1975, this covered hopper (the class were covered in a 1980-81 rebuild) has the same constructional features as those seen in *plate 86*. This is the last of the class of 20 which were sold to ICI Agricultural and carried prilled urea from Haverton Hill to the Ciba-Geigy resin adhesive works at Duxford. Livery is dark green with orange solebars and white lettering. They were later purchased by Cleveland Potash and work between Boulby and Tees Dock. Photographed at Middlesbrough on 1st June, 1989 (is).   A.T.

Plate 88. PR8245 was built in 1971 by Standard Wagon to design code PG 002D and is one of a new fleet of 45T g.l.w. open salt hoppers which were initially hired by BP Chemicals. Note the distinctive shape of the body, large open spoked handbrake wheel, sharply curved end ladders with a small platform and the long end stays. The 16ft wheelbase chassis is 30ft long and it has Oleo hydraulic buffers, double link taperleaf spring suspension and Instanter couplings. Livery is rusty grey with white lettering and it is covered by a white tarpaulin sheet with red lettering. (No.8251 is shown in *plate 56*). Photographed at Mossend on 11th August, 1988 (sc).   A.T.

Plate 89. BIS7987. TOPS coded PGA, this 51T g.l.w. hopper was constructed by Standard Wagon in 1981 to design code PG 018B. One of five in the class (7985-49) it is used to carry Chempure sand from Middleton Towers near Kings Lynn. These hoppers have no covers. Note the Gloucester floating axle suspension, Oleo buffers and end plates covering the control gear for the two pnuematically discharged hoppers. Livery is seen in *plate 65*. Photographed at Whitemoor on 7th April, 1991 (is).   S.J.

Plate 90. BIS7965. This covered hopper has similar specifications to the one in *plate 65* but it was built to design code PG 018C by W.H. Davis in 1981-2. The class of 11 (7950-60) have a 16ft wheelbase and are 26ft long with a one piece hopper cover. It carries Chempure sand from Middleton Towers to the glassworks at Cudworth in South Yorkshire and was photographed at Whitemoor on 7th April, 1991 (sr).

A.T.

Plate 91. BSRV12519 is one of the batch of 100 PGA covered hoppers, (12500-12599) which were built in 1979 by both Procor and BREL Shildon. The body has similar top doors to the previous wagon and there are protective end plates. Designed to carry pelletised iron ore or lime to Ravenscraig Steelworks, it has a load capacity of 38T and the body has six strengthening stays and two bottom discharge hoppers. Note the channel solebars, Oleo buffers and BSC Friction Pedestal suspension. After little use, they were scrapped in 1984. Photographed at Ardrossan on 1st September, 1979.   B.D.

Plate 92. STET18700-18729. This is one of the 30, 51T g.l.w. covered hoppers built to design code PA O11A by Standard Wagon in 1981 for Steetley Minerals for lime and dolime traffic between the quarries at Thrislington near Ferryhill and the Steetley plant near Hartlepool. Ground controlled air operated top covers mean no end inspection ladders or catwalks and the large side plates on the cream hopper body are an aid to shunting by ground-based Hymid wagon controllers. Note the Gloucester floating axle suspension on the 19ft wheelbase chassis and the white nameboard with black letters. Length is 29ft and TOPS code is PAA. Still at work in 1995, it was photographed at Thornaby in April 1989.   B.D.

Plate 93. PR8297 was built by Procor in 1975 and is TOPS coded PGA. Its 18ft 2ins wheelbase chassis has BSC Friction Pedestal suspension and there is a prominent handbrake wheel mounted on the wide flat solebar. Note the full width inspection platform at each end and the hand operated mechanism for the bottom discharge doors. Initially used for salt traffic for I.C.I. some were transferred to aggregate/limestone working but by 1992 this wagon and 24 others from the batch of 45 (8256-8300) were stored at Ely but it was one of 17 still in use in 1995. Livery is ARC yellow with black solebars and below and white lettering. Photographed at Stoke Gifford on 9th October, 1988 (is).   A.T.

Plate 94. PR 8901. From the third batch of salt hoppers built (8901-18) this wagon was produced by Procor in 1974-75 to the same design code - PG 007B as No.8297 in *plate 93*. Continuous use for salt traffic has led to much corrosion and most of the body and solebars are rusty in colour with a few light grey patches carrying black lettering on white patches or vice versa. No longer extant by 1995, it was photographed here at Runcorn on 12th August, 1989.   A.T.

Plate 95. AR 14212. TOPS coded PGA, this hopper is in use by ARC to carry aggregate. It was built by Charles Roberts & Co. Ltd. in 1972 and has the standard wheelbase of 16ft being 26ft long. Note the internal strengthening bars, BSC Friction Pedestal suspension, Oleo hydraulic buffers, central solebar-mounted control wheel for the hopper discharge and the end one for the handbrake. Livery is yellow body with blue panel carrying white lettering, black solebars and below with white lettering. Photographed at Radstock in Autumn 1978(is). D.L.

Plate 96. PR14096 is the first of the class of 56, 51T g.l.w. aggregate hopper wagons built to design code PG 006A by Charles Roberts & Co. Ltd. in 1975 and hired out via Procor. The solebar-mounted fleet plate has been removed, the hirer's name has been painted out and it carries no TOPS code. Note the small side strengtheners on the hopper body, end platforms with ladders and the brake pipes conducted along the side of the hopper. Livery is weathered grey-green body with black solebars all lettering being white. In store by 1992 and scrapped by 1995, it was photographed in solitary confinement with a red card at Didcot on 1st June, 1980. B.D.

Plate 97. AR14245 was built by Charles Roberts & Co. Ltd. in 1974 to design code PG 004A being one of the 40 in the class (14225-14264) owned by ARC initially but sold back to Procor and then hired by ARC! It has ladders and a platform at one end whilst at the other end the air brake cylinders etc. have a protective plate. Note the channel solebars and the Gloucester floating axle suspension. Livery is as in *plate 64*. but the ARC has faded. Photographed at the Isle of Grain on 2nd July, 1996. T.R.

Plate 98. PR14707 is the second of the class of 44 PGA hoppers built in 1978-79 by Procor and operated by ARC from Whatley. Only 6 were active by 1995 others being stored at Taunton where this one was photographed on 19th June, 1992. The hopper has a similar open top to AR 14245 in *plate 97*, but the top side plates are carried lower and it has platforms, ladders and protective plates at both ends. BSC Friction Pedestal suspension is fitted and it again has standard ARC livery 'caib' being in red on white. Photographed at Taunton on 19th June, 1992. A.T.

Plate 99. PR14731 is from the same class as No.14707 but to design code PG 013B, (the latter was to PG 013A). Note the big difference in the shape of the upper body other details are the same as is the livery and the photographic details (is). A.T.

Plate 100. PR14343 of design code PG 013E was built in 1980 by Procor and was one of 5 in the class of 56 (14333-14388) which were hired by ARC to carry aggregate from Whatley. The upper part of the hopper is different again and Gloucester floating axle suspension is used . Livery and photographic details as in *plate 99.* By 1995 it was still in store at Taunton (sr). A.T.

Plate 101. PR14325. A final look at ARC variations on the PGA 51T g.l.w. aggregate hopper theme! Most details of this design code - PG 016B are similar to the hopper in *plate100* but a different shape to the top of the body has led to differences in the end ladders and platforms. Its livery details etc. are as for No.14343 (sr). A.T.

Plate 102. PR14006 is one of the first batch of PGA hoppers used by Foster Yeoman which were built to design code PG 006A by Charles Roberts & Co. Ltd. in 1972, (25 hoppers, 14000-14024) and hired via Procor. It has standard dimensions of 16ft wheelbase and length of 26ft over buffers, tare weight is 12.7T and g.l.w. is 51T. This batch had the plain sloping sides to the hopper body, flat-sided solebars which slope down at the tops to the headstocks, a solid-centred handbrake control wheel, (replaced here) and the solebar-mounted board originally carried the Procor logo. It has Oleo buffers and BSC Friction Pedestal suspension. Note how the end ladders rise from the headstocks to a simple platform with no rear protection rail. Livery is as in *plate 54*. Photographed at Longport on 22nd June, 1993 it had been scrapped by 1995. S.J.

Plate 103. PR14185 was built to design code PG 013C by Procor in 1978-79 (14176-14197) and shows several major changes compared to PR 14006 in *plate 102*. The body shape has been changed and the end platforms are now accessed from side ladders. The end plates are more robust and support the end platforms and the body is supported by four 'T'-shaped struts which are also found on the hopper ends. Channel solebars are now in favour and it carries standard Yeoman livery. Working from Merehead, it was photographed at Hoo Junction on 9th June, 1989 and was still active in 1995(is).   T.R.

Plate 104. PR14320 is the first of the small class of 4 PGA hoppers built to design code PG 015A by Procor in 1979. There are few constructional differences between this one and No.14185 in *plate 103* but this design should be noted for introducing Gloucester floating axle suspension to Foster Yeoman hoppers. The light grey parts of the livery have faded almost to white here and the name panel is showing signs of wear. Photographed in store at Taunton on 19th June,1992 - sold to Grant Rail by March 1999.

                                                                                                    A.T.

Plate 105. BRT14617. Built by Standard Wagon in 1974, this PGA hopper is from the class of 55 (14600-14654), the first 27 of which were hired by the Staveley Lime Company from the British Railway Traffic & Electric Co. to work between its quarry at Dove Holes near Buxton and depots at Salford and Liverpool. It has a wheelbase of 16ft and its end platforms and ladders are similar to some of the other early PGA hoppers illustrated. Livery is pale blue body with maroon lettering and it was photographed at Peak Forest in October 1978. All the class were in store at Ely or Peak Forest in 1992 and by 1995 those at Peak Forest had gone.   D.L.

Plate 106. TAMC14682 is one of the class of 33 hoppers built by Standard Wagon to design code PG 006E in 1974 for Tarmac Roadstone to work from their quarries near Buxton. By 1979 they had moved to Cliffe Hill and by 1995 they were operating from Whatley. When this one was photographed at Maidstone West in Summer 1977, they had been taken over by Procor. Note the deep flush solebars, BSC Friction Pedestal suspension and the similarity between this design and PR 14688 in *plate 64*. Livery is white body with a brown panel and solebars which have white lettering and running gear is black (sr).   D.L.

Plate 107. TAMC14863 is from the class of hoppers 14840-14870 which were built by Procor in 1979-80. Still 26ft long with a wheelbase of 16ft these hoppers have the standard channel solebars, Gloucester floating axle suspension and four side strengthening stays to the hopper instead of the five seen in the previous wagons. The body has changed to the style seen in *plate 101* (built to design code PG 016B whereas No.14863 is to PG 016A) so that the end ladders are continued up from the solebars - note the heavy duty buffers. Livery is chocolate brown overall with white lettering - the Tarmac motif has black letters edged in white. Photographed at Stratford on 13th June, 1996 (sr). T.R.

Plate 108. BSTE18052 is one of the 115 (18000-18114) 51T g.l.w. (37T load) limestone hoppers which were built for British Steel Teeside by Standard Wagon in 1975. 27ft long with a wheelbase of 16ft 6ins these wagons have automatic bottom discharge with HAA mgr type operating mechanism and the channel solebars are supported on BSC Primary Coil suspension. The hopper has a narrow top loading aperture and pairs of long supporting stays at each end. Livery is grey body - very heavily stained with limestone here - with white lettering. The British Steel symbol is blue on white and the solebars and below are black. Operation is in block trains carrying limestone from Hardendale near Shap, (originally from Redmire) to the blast furnaces at Lackenby. Photographed at Tees Yard on 21st March, 1993 (sr). S.J.

Plate 109. SRW18506. When some of the hoppers seen in the previous plate became redundant in 1982, Standard Wagon purchased them and after modification for general use, they were numbered in the SRW 18500-18529 series. SRW 18506 was originally BSTE 18050. By 1992 they were in store at Tinsley and by 1995 they were at Aldwarke or R.F.S Doncaster, one (No.18509) being at Carnforth. Livery is white overall with black lettering except for 'Railease' which is blue. Note how the shape of the hopper has been changed, there are added ladders and an inspection platform at each end and the discharge mechanism is different. Photographed at Tinsley, Sheffield on 21st September, 1991 (sc). A.T.

Plate 110. APCM19559. Portland cement and other special types require small amounts of gypsum, (calcium sulphate) for their chemical setting which may not be present in the clay and chalk used to make the cement. This batch of 46T g.l.w hoppers (19551-19589) were built by BREL Shildon in 1970 to carry gypsum between the British Gypsum mine at Mountfield and Northfleet Cement Works. Based on the BR m.g.r. hopper, it is 29ft long with two sets of bottom discharge doors. Note the strengthening supports to the galvanised steel hopper body. Photographed at Brixton in Winter 1980-81 (sc). D.L.

Plate 111. APCM19587 is from the same batch of PGA hoppers as No.19559 but here we see the other end of the wagon with discharge gear, brake cylinder and access ladder. Note the pipework carried along the channel solebar and the long link suspension. Wheelbase is 16ft 6ins and livery is galvanised steel body, black supports, solebars and below with white lettering except for the hopper number which is black. Photographed at Tonbridge on 5th May, 1991 (sc). A.T.

Plate 112. I.C.I.M.19074 is one of the 71T g.l.w. bogie limestone hoppers which were numbered 19000-19151 and were built by Charles Roberts & Co. Ltd. to design code JG 001A at various times between 1936 and 1953. Vacuum braked with a cylinder on the platform at each end, this one still runs on the original diamond framed bogies. The hopper is divided into two compartments braced with six substantial side stays as well as two at each end. Livery is grey with white lettering, (initially they were pale green with black lettering). Photographed at Chinley in Autumn 1976. D.L.

Plate 113. I.C.I.M.19064 is similar to No.19074 in plate 112 but this one has the later Gloucester plate back bogies which were fitted to the post-war built wagons and as replacements to the earlier ones. Note the vacuum pipe running down the side. Livery is brownish grey on a wet day. These hoppers ran in block trains carrying limestone from Tunstead near Buxton to the I.C.I. plant at Northwich where it is used in the manufacture of sodium carbonate. No longer in use on this service and 37 were scrapped at Attercliffe in July 1998. Photographed at Buxton on 17th December, 1989.   A.T.

Plate 114. BSSH13124 is one of the unfitted hoppers which were built by Charles Roberts Co. Ltd. in l953 - to the same design as the I.C.I ones, for John Summers (later the British Steel Corporation) for transporting imported iron ore from Bidston Dock on the Wirral to the blast furnaces at Shotton near Connah's Quay. The plant closed in 1983 and the redundant hoppers were purchased by I.C.I. Photographed at Bidston in Winter 1979-80.   D.L.

Plate 115. I.C.I.M.19155 is one of the 13 former British Steel Corporation hoppers put into service after refurbishment by I.C.I. (the serviced batch was 19152-19164).The major alterations were the addition of vacuum brakes and roller bearings. Livery is light grey overall with white lettering - 'I.C.I.' being raised letters. Photographed at Buxton on 17th December, 1989.　　　　　　　　　　　　　　　A.T.

Plate 116. REDA16079. This is one of the inner hopper wagons from the self-discharge train sets operated by Redland Aggregates. Discharge is via a clam shell door arrangement onto a continuous conveyor belt which carries the aggregate to the end of the train where the unloading station is situated *(see plate 119)*. This is a Mark II inner (16057-16081), of design code PH 019B built by Powell Dufflyn in 1989. It has a tare weight of 13T and a load capacity of 38T, length being 25ft 1ins and wheelbase 15ft 8ins. Livery is light green overall with grey solebars and below. Lettering is white except for the TOPS panel which is black, Redland being on a red background and 'AGGREGATES' on a grey one. Photographed at Peterborough on 7th April, 1991.　　　　　　　　　　　　　　　S.J.

Plate 117. REDA16309 is the last of the batch of five self-discharge train Mark II power inner hoppers built to design code PH 022B in 1990. It is 29ft 5ins long with a wheelbase of 16ft 9ins. Tare weight is 15T and load capacity 36T. At the lefthand end we see the Lister Petter HL 4008 diesel engine which is used to power the conveyor belt and the hydraulic system. Livery and photographic details are as in *plate 116*.

S.J.

Plate 118. REDA16223 is a Mark II outer hopper (16214-16223) from the self-discharge train built by Powell Duffryn Standard in 1990 to design code PH 021D. It has the same livery as in *plate 116* but construction is slightly different - the hopper bottom is inclined to the right to allow the conveyor belt to extend and discharge onto the unloading station. It also has the drawbar coupling at the inner end and a conventional coupling and buffers at the outer end. Note the channel solebars, small handbrake lever and Gloucester Pedestal suspension. Tare weight is 15.25T, load capacity 35.8T, wheelbase l5ft 8ins and length over buffers 29ft 5ins. Photographic details as in *plate 116*. S.J.